Managing Anger

60 Simple Ways to Control Anger and Feel Calmer

A.B. Alin

loss due to the information herein, either directly or indirectly.

The information in this book is for informational purposes only and is universal as so. The presentation of the information is without contract or any type of guarantee assurance.

The trademarks that are used are without any consent, and the publication of the trademark is without permission or backing by the trademark owner. All trademarks and brands within this book are for clarifying purposes only and are the owned by the owners themselves, not affiliated with this document.

Table of Contents

Free Bonus 1

Introduction 3

Part 1: Understanding Anger 6

Chapter 1: Getting to Know Anger 7

    Causes of Anger 8

    Types of Anger...10

    Common Misconceptions 16

    Quick Summary: 17

Chapter 2: Signs of Anger 19

    Warning Signs 19

    When is Anger a Problem? 20

    Why Do Some People Get Angrier Than Others?
   21

    Quick Summary: 22

Part 2: Impact of Anger....................................23

Chapter 3: Effects of Anger 25

    Increases the Risk of Heart Attacks 25

    Increases the Risk of Stroke............................... 26

    Weakens the Immune System........................... 26

Leads to Depression...27

Damages Your Lungs..27

Ruins Relationships... 28

Worsens Anxiety 28

Quick Summary: 29

Chapter 4: Benefits of Managing Anger 31

Good Judgment...31

Less Stress...31

Fewer Disputes and Conflicts 31

Better Communication 32

Healthy Relationships 32

Take Responsibility... 33

Empathy.. 33

Quick Summary: 33

Part 3: Managing Anger 34

Chapter 5: What is Anger Management? 35

The 3 Most Effective Methods............................. 36

Chapter 6: Anger Management Strategies 39

Preventive/Long-Term Strategies 39

Immediate/Short-Term Strategies 51

Quick Summary: 60

Chapter 7: Specific Strategies 61

Dealing with Internalized Anger 61

Dealing with Anger in a Relationship 64

Dealing with Anger at Work 67

Quick Summary: 70

Chapter 8: Confronting Angry People 71

Maintain a Calm Demeanor 71

Quick Summary: 73

Chapter 9: What If the Techniques Don't
Work? 75

Pitfalls to Avoid 76

If You Get Angry 76

Quick Summary: 78

Conclusion 79

Quick List of Anger Management Strategies 80

Thanks for Reading 85

Free Bonus

As a way of saying thank you for downloading my book, I wanted to offer you two FREE resources to help you get started in managing your anger. My Anger Control Plan template will assist you in crafting a carefully thought out plan to overcome anger in all of its forms.

Without a way of tracking your anger management goals and progress, you won't be able to fully utilize any anger control plan. This is why I've included an Anger Log with your gift. With this template, you can record your episodes of anger and be able to assess the effectiveness of your anger management strategy and make improvements as necessary. So...what are you waiting for?

Get instant access to these incredible resources for **FREE** by going here:

https://tinyurl.com/free-anger-control-plan/

Introduction

Anger is a powerful emotion that could have devastating consequences. So why should you let it take over your life? Why should you just accept it and do nothing while it destroys you, your family, and your career? The good news is that anger, although overwhelming, is an emotion YOU can manage. You CAN change your ways and discover how to be in control of your temper and live a stress-free life without regrets.

In America alone, almost 22 million people have severe anger issues. It's time that we recognize the seriousness of this emotion. It's time that we discover how to diffuse it, manage it, and express it in a healthy way.

In this step-by-step guide, I'll shed some light on how to do just that. You'll discover what anger is and its causes and negative effects on your health and relationships. You'll find a catalog of over 60 simple, but effective strategies to overcome different types of anger—no matter how extreme or minor they might be. These are strategies that anybody can use in any situation. Included are also specific strategies for dealing with anger in relationships and at work.

Through the information in this book, you'll have a better understanding of your own anger issues and be able to create an individual plan to manage it with easy to apply methods that you can refer to at any time. What you'll learn here is from years of extensive research and life experiences coupled with data from actual studies. However, I won't be referencing scientific research, except in rare instances, or using jargon since this is meant to be a simple and practical guide and not a research paper.

My goal with this book is simple, I want to equip you with as many tools as possible to help you combat this powerful emotion and be the best version of yourself. It's never too late and I know you can do it because you won half the battle when you decided to take massive action and download this book. Before long, we'll jump straight into the fun stuff and work on expanding your repertoire of anger coping strategies. After you're done with this book, you will have all the tools you need to overcome anger, to be able to face the daily challenges of life with control and calmness, to be able to communicate peacefully with your loved ones without losing your temper. If you've had this burning desire all along but have been unable to achieve it, then read on and implement the tactics in this book.

Part 1: Understanding Anger

"Anger is a feeling that makes your mouth work faster than your mind."

Chapter 1:
Getting to Know Anger

The goal of this section is to help you become familiar with anger and specifically, your anger so you can be prepared to create an appropriate plan to manage it in Chapter 6. So, what is anger exactly? Anger is a normal feeling of displeasure that comes instinctively to everybody. People respond with this emotion when they perceive danger, threat, surprise, loneliness, or stress.

Have you ever seen a dog bare its teeth at you when you step on its paw? The dog does this because it perceives you as a threat. People also show similar emotions when they recognize danger. Their mind stimulates the adrenal glands to release adrenaline. It's a survival mechanism that helps you assess the situation and fight or flee from it.

If you manage your anger right, you can make positive changes to your life and learn to handle situations with ease. Mismanaged anger, on the other hand, complicates situations further. When one's anger is out of control or misdirected, it leads to poor decision making and causes problems in relationships both at work and at home.

Causes of Anger

Anger can be caused by many different things. It could be due to culture, family background, genetics, trauma, hormonal changes, mental illnesses, or just daily life challenges. Personality types also affect the kinds of things that can trigger a person's anger.

Research suggests that family background and culture affect the way we perceive anger. We learn how to show anger through them as well. Some cultures are open to expressing their anger, while some tend to suppress theirs. There are also gender differences in cultures when it comes to what is considered appropriate. Most cultures lean toward the idea that men can show their anger while women have to suppress theirs. Men from such cultures tend to lash out more than women.

Sometimes, anger is situational and is caused by certain events like someone driving in front of you at a slower speed or your car breaking down on the road. At times the anger we feel is not related to any person or situation.

It might be because of fatigue or illness. For instance, we might be more irritable after a long day of work. Or it could be caused by starvation or being "hangry." This is when a person becomes irritable and angry due to hunger. Doctors explain that the reason this happens is because the blood sugar drops when a person doesn't eat for a long time, which then releases cortisol, a hormone that can cause aggression in certain people. This is also the case with diabetics when their blood sugar is low, they become irritable and quick to get angry.

Stress is another common trigger. One could be stressed about the direction of his career or not being able to find work. Such a worry can easily turn into rage. Familial problems such as breakups, divorces, arguments are major causes of stress and anger as well. Anger caused by those closest to us can be extremely nerve-wracking. Anger could also be caused by hormonal changes such as premenstrual syndrome, menopause, and pregnancy in women. Imbalances in testosterone levels can similarly lead to increased irritability and anger in men.

Sometimes suppressed emotions like fear, anxiety, and sadness transform into anger.

Sadness for instance, when it's continuously ignored and unexpressed, manifests itself through anger causing a normally peaceful person to become furious with rage. This is why it's critical that a person tries to discover the cause of his sadness and then allow himself to feel and show it without judging it. This will help the person let go of the negative emotions.

Types of Anger

People have different forms of anger. The way they express their anger will also vary depending on their circumstances and mood. It's important to understand your anger type so that you can know how to better manage it. There are many classifications for the different kinds of anger, but in this section, we'll list the common types.

1. Constructive Anger

Constructive or assertive anger is a positive way of expressing anger. This is usually the result of a successful anger management program. It means being confident with your words and effective at communicating your emotions without raising your voice or insulting others. It means considering the feelings and perspectives of others. It likewise means expressing your anger in a positive way to make positive changes.

2. Passive Anger

This form of anger is common in men. They avoid confrontation and display anger indirectly. He might use methods like sarcasm or stubbornness to coverup his feelings. He might also deny that he's angry and refuse to talk about his emotions. Passive-aggressive anger is especially dangerous to relationships as it blocks communication. It's the most difficult to identify and control. One of the best ways to overcome this kind of anger is to become self-aware of one's behavior and then create a plan to better cope with the triggers. More on this in Chapter 7.

3. Behavioral Anger

People with behavioral anger are very confrontational. They often lash out at the person who angered them with rudeness and possibly even violence. They may throw or break things. This form of anger is unpredictable and has many negative personal and social effects. With this type of anger problem, it's best to just stop and walk away. Take a moment to breathe and calm yourself down.

Disengage from the situation and distract yourself with an enjoyable activity that'll put you in a good mood.

4. Verbal Anger

Verbal anger is not as dangerous as behavioral anger, but it can still cause overwhelming emotional damage. People with this type of anger intentionally use threats, yelling, mockery, and blaming to hurt people. And they usually feel guilty and apologetic afterward. If you suffer from this, refrain from talking and walk away. Take some time to cool down and gather your thoughts.

5. Chronic Anger

Chronic anger is an ongoing resentment of people, anger towards oneself, and frustration with certain situations. They hate the world and they hate everybody and everything in it. They're quick to explode but can calm down just as easily. If you have this form of anger, try to spend some time to understand the root cause of your anger. Once you do this, you can then work to resolve the inner conflicts and change your aggressive behaviors.

6. Judgmental Anger

Judgmental anger is a reaction to another person's faults or some perceived injustice. It's a form of justified fury because, according to the angry person, he or she's morally superior. This type of anger is usually accompanied by low self-esteem. They try to feel better about themselves by bringing others down. Due to their offensive and inconsiderate behavior, they alienate themselves from others. If you suffer from this, try to be understanding of others and learn to look at situations from different angles. Putting yourself in their shoes will allow you to consider their thoughts and feelings and how you should respond to them.

7. Overwhelmed Anger

This often occurs when a person feels that a situation is beyond their control. They feel like they've taken on too much responsibility. This results in feelings of frustration and hopelessness. They eventually can't hold it in anymore and explode with anger causing harm to themselves and others. It may also be caused by an inability to cope with stress. If you experience this type of anger, you have to reach out for help. Let your loved ones know you need support. Talk to them about your problems. Don't be afraid to ask them to help you with your chores or to babysit the children. Managing your sources of stress can help you feel at ease and regain a sense of emotional control. Also, seek professional advice to help you better manage your emotions.

8. Avoidant Anger

Since anger is often considered a negative emotion, most people keep all their anger bottled up. This is especially the case with cultures that have gender biases. These cultures say that women have to always suppress their anger. However, suppressing anger could lead to increased tension. When this anger multiplies, the person might explode one day and lash out at the wrong people. To better cope with this, a person needs to learn constructive ways to release anger and tension. They need to improve their communication skills so that they can effectively voice their concerns.

9. Retaliatory Anger

People display this form of anger when they're confronted or insulted by others. Most people react this way when they believe someone wronged them. Retaliatory anger is intentional, and it aims to intimidate anybody who asserts any control over the person suffering from it. This form of anger only escalates tensions. If you suffer from this, as soon as you notice your anger escalating, stop and get yourself out of the situation. Give yourself time to think about how you want to express yourself. Also, learn to let go and forgive others instead of seeking revenge.

10. Self-Abusive Anger

This is also known as internalized anger. It can have lasting damaging effects on a person's mental and physical health. People display this form of anger when they're ashamed or feel guilty about something and feel they need to punish themselves. When such a person feels unworthy, hopeless, ashamed, or humiliated, she will tend to internalize those feelings and express her anger through self-harm, negative self-talk, substance use, and aggression towards others. She may also lash out at the people she loves because she wants to mask her feelings and emotions. To overcome this, a person has to learn techniques to change the way they think about themselves and try to focus on the present instead of the past.

As you can see, anger can take many forms and be expressed in many different ways. The first step in learning to overcome anger is to know the type and cause of your personal anger. We'll look at coping strategies in Part 3 of this book.

Common Misconceptions

1. "Anger is bad."

Anger is an emotion that's not bad in and of itself. Even though we feel bad when we're angry, it helps us assess a situation and sometimes stand up for ourselves or others in need.

2. "Venting anger helps to get it all out.'

It has been proven that using physical or verbal means to "let off steam" is the worst strategy. These methods may increase the person's anger and hostility and it trains them to see "venting" as the only way to manage their anger.

3. "Ignoring makes the anger go away."

Anger is a reflex to a situation that is perceived as dangerous. Ignoring it doesn't help. It only suppresses the anger which could lead to passive aggression, lashing out, stress, psychological problems, or health issues.

Although anger is a feeling we can't control, we can, however, control our responses to it. If our response is to lash out or scream, then we need to learn to stop and make rational choices.

4. "Suppress your anger."

Expressing anger in a healthy and respectful manner is a good thing. However, when we explode and react aggressively or internalize the anger, then this is when it leads to problems.

Quick Summary:

- **Anger**: A normal but strong feeling of displeasure.

- **Causes of anger**: They include family background, culture, personal triggers, stress, exhaustion, and hormonal imbalances.

- **Types of Anger:** There are many forms of anger and you must understand your type so that you can be better equipped to manage it.

- **Some common misconceptions:**

    ○ *"Anger is bad."*

- o *"Venting anger helps to let it out."*
- o *"Ignoring it makes it go away."*
- o *"Suppress your anger."*

Chapter 2:
Signs of Anger

To better understand your personal anger and how it manifests itself. Ask yourself these questions:

- How do frustrating situations affect me?
- How do my responses affect other people?
- How do I know when I'm angry?

Warning Signs

Most people experience numerous emotional, behavioral, and physical cues to indicate when they're about to become upset. Below are some common warning signs:

Physical Cues:

- Trembling or shaking
- Grinding your teeth or clenching your jaw
- Feeling hot in the face and neck
- Headache
- Increased and rapid heart rate
- • Sweating in your palms and underarms
- Stomachache

- Dizziness

Emotional Cues:

- Irritation
- Depression or sadness
- Guilt
- Resentment

Behavioral Cues:

- Acting in an abusive manner
- Smoking or drinking
- Yelling
- Crying
- Rubbing your head
- Pacing
- Becoming sarcastic
- Losing your sense of humor

When is Anger a Problem?

All human beings experience anger in some form or shape but it can become a problem when it happens regularly and in high intensity and leads to behaviors like verbal and physical aggression. In other words, when we can't control this feeling and express it in a healthy way, we have an anger management problem. If you're in doubt about whether or not you have an anger issue, refer to a professional for an accurate diagnosis.

Why Do Some People Get Angrier Than Others?

For some people, any small misunderstanding can lead to an angry outburst. There are others that don't show much of their anger but are constantly grumpy or irritable. And the ones with passive-aggressive anger simply choose to withdraw socially or refrain from talking.

The reason why some people become angry more easily than others is that they have a lower tolerance for stress or frustration. They feel that they don't have to be subjected to annoyance, frustration, and inconvenience. They become infuriated if they're in a situation that seems unjust or frustrating. For instance, they may dislike it if someone was to correct them for making a mistake.

So, what makes people behave this way?

One cause may be biological or genetic. Research shows that some children are born sensitive, easily angered, and irritable. Another cause may be sociocultural. Most people regard anger as a negative emotion. People are told it's okay to express depression, anxiety, and other emotions, but they can't express anger. It's for this reason people don't learn to channel or handle anger constructively. Research similarly shows that family background plays a major role, and people who come from families that have high tempers are more likely to be irritable, disruptive, and lack the skill to effectively manage their emotions.

Quick Summary:

- **Common Symptoms**: Trembling, grinding one's teeth, feeling hot in the face and neck, increased heart rate, irritation, pacing, and yelling.

- **You must understand your warning signs** so that you can create a plan to diffuse your anger before it intensifies.

- **Some people get angry more easily than others due to** low tolerance to stressors, genetics, culture, and family background.

Part 2: Impact of Anger

"If you're patient in one moment of anger, you'll escape a hundred days of sorrow."

Chapter 3:
Effects of Anger

Anger can be good for you at times if you express it in a healthy way. Unhealthy episodes of anger, however, wreak havoc on your mind, body, and social life. Below are some of the negative consequences of anger.

Increases the Risk of Heart Attacks

Angry outbursts have a significant impact on your heart. According to Chris Aiken, the director of the Mood Treatment Center in North Carolina and an instructor in the clinical psychiatry department at Wake Forest University, the chances of having a heart attack or cardiac arrest increase after an angry outburst. Repressed or internalized anger also leads to heart attacks and other diseases. When you go to great lengths to control your anger or repress it, you stress your heart. A recent study showed that short-tempered people were at greater risk of coronary disease compared to those who were not. If you want to protect your heart, you must learn to manage your negative emotions and thoughts before they destroy you.

Speaking about your feelings or dealing with anger constructively will reduce the risk of a heart attack.

Increases the Risk of Stroke

If you lash out frequently, you're at a higher risk of stroke. A study showed that people who had frequent angry outbursts had a higher chance of having a stroke due to bleeding or a blood clot in the brain, especially during the first two hours after an episode. People with an aneurysm were at a higher risk of having a stroke after an angry outburst.

Weakens the Immune System

If you're constantly mad about something, you feel sick more often. A study conducted by Harvard University found that people showed a dip in the antibody immunoglobulin A when they thought about an event or situation that led to anger. This antibody is your body's first line of defense against any infection, and a constant decline in this antibody can greatly weaken your immune system.

Leads to Depression

Research shows that depression is linked to angry outbursts and aggression, especially in men. According to Aiken, men are passive-aggressive, which means they tend to worry about the situation but never take any action. His advice is that people with depression should focus on controlling their temper. They also need to keep themselves busy so that they don't have much time to think. Any activity that absorbs a person's attention is a good way to cure anger.

Damages Your Lungs

Hostility and anger can harm your lungs. Harvard University conducted a study to determine the relationship between hostility, anger, and lung function. The team studied 670 men for 8 years and measured their anger and hostility levels. They also looked at how a change in these levels affected their lung function. Men with a high reading on the anger and hostility scale had terrible lung capacity, and this increased the risk of respiratory problems.

Ruins Relationships

Anger is part of all relationships, but if your anger is severe and mismanaged, it could have negative lasting effects on the people closest to you. If you frequently explode on your partner or loved ones, they'll come to fear you, resent you, and possibly even leave you. This will also cause them to become frustrated and angry with you which will lead to a cycle of vicious angry exchange patterns. Everybody has their limits and if you keep lashing out at them and verbally abusing them, they'll eventually walk away.

Worsens Anxiety

If you constantly worry about your life or your current situation, you'll be angry all the time. It's important to note that anger and anxiety are closely related. A study published in 2012 in the Cognitive Behavior Therapy Journal showed that anger always worsens any symptoms of anxiety, depression, or other psychological issues. The study also showed that people with Generalized Anxiety Disorder are always angry and hostile and that they have trouble expressing their anger in an effective way.

Stress affects general health, and if you're angry and stressed all the time, your health and well-being will gradually deteriorate. This is why it's important to learn how to manage and express anger productively. The good news is that you **can** learn to control your anger and research has proven this. We'll go more in detail about exactly how in Chapter 5.

Quick Summary:

- **Effects of anger:** Increased risk of stroke and heart attack, weak immune system, depression, damaged lungs, and increased anxiety and stress.

- Not treating your anger issues can have long term negative effects on you and those around you.

Chapter 4:
Benefits of Managing Anger

Anger issues negatively affect all aspects of a person's life including those around the angry person. And learning to manage and cope with it can lead to better overall well-being and many positive changes such as:

Good Judgment

When angry, your judgment will be impaired, and you will make poor decisions. Once you learn to manage your anger, you can control your thoughts and actions which will in turn help you exercise better judgment.

Less Stress

When you learn to control your anger better, you find it easier to manage stress and avoid getting overwhelmed.

Fewer Disputes and Conflicts

When you have an anger problem, you find yourself constantly engaging in disputes with others over simple matters. As you learn techniques and strategies to control your anger, you will argue less and learn to let go of things and not look at disagreements as personal attacks.

Better Communication

Often, people tend to feel angry because of minor misunderstandings due to a lack of communication. Good communication skills help to prevent such misunderstandings. When you channel and express your anger in a productive way, it becomes easier to communicate with the person you're angry with and it allows you to be more open-minded.

Healthy Relationships

Another benefit of successfully managing one's anger is that it allows a person to build better and stronger relationships. Close family members are often the victims of mismanaged anger. Having a grip on one's negative emotions can help a person avoid harming himself and his loved ones.

Take Responsibility

When you control your anger, you learn to look at situations from a neutral standpoint and identify whether or not you're at fault. And if it is indeed your fault, you learn to accept it and apologize.

Empathy

Through anger management, you learn to empathize with how the other person feels. You look at the situation from their point of view to better understand their thoughts and reasoning behind their behavior. Through empathy, you'll have fewer conflicts and misunderstandings with others.

Quick Summary:

- A successful anger management program can help improve all aspects of a person's life and lead to positive lifestyle changes.

- **Benefits of Managing Anger**: Good judgment, less stress, fewer disputes, better communication, healthy relationships, and empathy.

Part 3: Managing Anger

"Learn to control your anger before it dictates the path you take in life"

Chapter 5:
What is Anger Management?

Anger is not always a negative emotion, but it can be problematic if it leads to outbursts, physical altercations, and aggression. Therefore, it's important to learn to manage it so that that you avoid doing or saying something you're going to regret.

When anger is mismanaged, it can have grave consequences. But what is mismanaged anger? Mismanaged anger is anger that you misdirect or can't control. Your inability to control it might frustrate you even further. So not addressing it immediately will only cause further damage.

You have to learn healthy ways of expressing your anger. This is where Anger Management comes in. It helps you identify why and how you get angry and then provides appropriate methods or ways to express and cope with your anger. Research has proven that anger management does work. You **can** control your anger using effective anger management strategies.

The 3 Most Effective Methods

According to Deffenbacher, the three strategies that have the most data and research to support them are:

1. **Relaxation Techniques:** Specialists train patients to use special words or visualize calming images to relax in an anger causing situation.

2. **Skill Development:** The patient is taught to focus on developing certain behaviors to help manage his anger. For example, if a woman is abusive towards her partner, she's encouraged to improve her relationship skills.

3. **Cognitive Behavioral Therapy:** Methods are used to change the way a person behaves, thinks, and reacts to anger. These are based on notions that your feelings, behaviors, and thoughts are all deeply connected. Certain thoughts and behaviors can affect your emotions, negatively or positively. Changing the negative thoughts into positive or reasonable ones can help one change the negative reactions.

The following chapters will provide a step-by-step guide on how to manage anger using a catalog of different strategies based on these three methods.

Chapter 6:
Anger Management Strategies

Preventive/Long-Term Strategies

Anger is often caused by an underlying issue such as mental disorders, trauma, fatigue, stress, or drug abuse and is not directly related to the trigger. Addressing these causes can decrease the outbursts of anger. However, sometimes anger has to be treated as an isolated issue. Regardless, it's important to practice long-term strategies or positive lifestyle changes to get anger under control. Below is a quick list of proven interventions to prevent anger.

#1: Be Aware

Before you can act, you have to become aware of your anger and recognize it in yourself. Reflect on the damage and harm it's caused you physically, emotionally, and socially. Use that to motivate yourself to change and act immediately to control your temper before it causes you or others any more harm. As the saying goes, "suffering drives change." Being mindful and aware of the reality of your anger and accepting that you have a problem is the first step to overcoming anger.

#2: Identify Your "Why"

To accomplish anything in life, you need a big enough motive or a powerful reason to drive you towards fulfilling that desired goal—this is your "why." Having a clearly defined "why" will allow you to push through difficulties and obstacles that come your way. A strong passion can lead to great results. Like any other habit or goal, developing anger managing habits require a "why." Ask yourself: Why do I need to manage my anger? How will my life change if I learn to control my temper? What will happen if I continue to let my angry emotions take over?

For some, their big "why" or motive in controlling their anger might be to attain self-discipline, for others, it might simply be to become a better father or spouse. Before you continue with the rest of this book, get out a piece of paper, and define your "why." Post it where you can easily review it every day; this could be the background image for your phone, or next to your desk at work, or somewhere in your car. Learning to change one's angry behaviors is a challenge and most people give up because they never defined their "why's" in the initial stage. This is a very important tip and you can apply it to improve other aspects of your life.

#3: Learn Your Triggers & Signs

Try to also identify the things that anger you (i.e., your triggers). Common triggers include traffic jams, long lines, excessive tiredness, and snarky comments. Understanding your triggers and the intensity of your anger for each trigger will help you anticipate your anger and plan your responses accordingly. Making a list of your triggers is a critical step in learning to manage your anger.

After recognizing the causes of your anger, the next step is to understand the cues that your body gives you as you're about to get angry. A person doesn't experience anger unexpectedly, it doesn't go from zero to rage. There are warning signs and recognizing these signs is a vital step in learning how to control your temper. Jot down your warning signs, both physical and emotional, next to your triggers on the same piece of paper. You can find examples of common signs in Chapter 2.

#4: Make Goals

Make specific goals to manage your different triggers or situations. Think of the goals as your desired behaviors in response to the causes of your anger. For example, let's say one of your triggers is your spouse insulting you, your goal might be to take deep breaths, remain calm, and refrain from insulting him back. Create detailed goals for each of your triggers and in the next tip, we'll combine all of the previous tips to create an action plan.

#5: Create a Control Plan

After specifying your triggers, warning signs, and creating goals, the next step is to plan how you're going to control your anger. How will you keep your cool and refrain from exploding? What strategies will you use to maintain your anger arousal? How will you use these strategies? Combining all of this information is essentially what an anger management plan is.

To create your anger control plan, follow these steps:

1. Identify your triggers and the level of your anger.

2. Identify your anger arousal signs.
3. Create goals for tackling each trigger.
4. Decide on which tools to employ to diffuse your anger.
5. Keep track of your progress.
6. Review your control plan every morning.

To help you create a well-defined control plan to manage your anger, don't forget to check out my FREE templates in the bonus section of the beginning of the book.

With the correct plan, you'll be able to calmly respond instead of reacting to triggers. And once you learn to successfully implement your control plan for all your triggers, you'll have mastered anger management.

Another tip to help you stick to your anger management plan is to involve others. Let your loved ones know of your anger issues and your plan for managing it. Ask them to support you and hold you accountable.

#6: Practice Your Response

Rehearsing your response to each trigger is key to implement your anger control plan. After deciding on which strategy to use for your triggers, practice, and role-play the different scenarios and the appropriate responses in your head or in front of a mirror. This will allow you to be prepared so when you're faced with a trigger, you'll be in better shape to control your temper and prevent any outbursts.

#7: Track Your Progress

To successfully evaluate the success of your anger management plan, you too need to record every episode of anger in an anger log. Record when and where it happened, the cause, how you felt, and what anger management strategy you implemented. The benefit of this is that it allows you to determine which strategies worked more effectively in managing your anger and which ones didn't help. With this information, you can plan better going forward. Also, tracking your feelings during a situation of anger can help you better understand and change the emotions and thoughts that contribute to your anger. This is vital information that you can use for the cognitive-behavioral therapies mentioned earlier.

#8: Control Your Thoughts

Challenge your negative thoughts and don't allow them to cloud your vision. Negative thoughts are known triggers so replace them with positive ones. For example, let's say you're stuck in a traffic jam. If you tell yourself the jam is going to ruin your entire day, you're going to become more frustrated as focusing on triggers only increases your anger. Focus instead on why the situation occurred. Since there are many cars on the road, there was bound to be a traffic jam. Shifting your thoughts this way can help you accept the unfavorable situation and feel better.

#9: Reward Yourself

Be proud of yourself every time you succeed in managing your anger. Acknowledge your efforts and treat yourself whenever you successfully control your temper in a stressful situation. Doing this will motivate you to keep going forward in your battle against anger. And remember these successes to encourage yourself to not give up if or when you do fail.

#10: Exercise Regularly

Exercising has been proven to reduce anger and calm one's nerves. It's also been proven to relieve tension and stress, two common causes of anger. Make it a goal to exercise regularly to improve your mental and physical well-being.

#11: Eat Well

A well-balanced diet consisting of the correct amount of healthy fat, protein, carbs, nutrients, and vitamins plays a key role in the well-being of your brain and the regulation of your emotions. Studies have shown that diets lacking adequate amounts of carbs, or nutrients like omega-3 fatty acids may lead to mood disorders and increased anger. Similarly, university studies have proven that diets high in trans fats increase irritability.

#12: Sleep Well

Poor sleep and anger inversely affect each other. Research has confirmed that inadequate sleep increases feelings of anger while anger issues lead to poor sleep. Lack of good sleep will cause fatigue and increased irritability. It also impairs your ability to control anger as well as how quickly you become angry. It adversely affects your overall mood and leads to a host of mental issues.

To ensure that you get quality sleep: exercise daily, eat well and try to sleep a minimum of 7 hours every night. Following these three tips (regular exercise, healthy diet, quality sleep) can help you live a healthy lifestyle and promote feelings of serenity and joy.

#13: Manage Your Stress

As mentioned before, stress is a common cause of anger and the more stressed a person is, the more irritable they'll be. As part of a successful anger management plan, getting stress under control is a must. Stress management is a lifestyle change that can bring many other positive benefits to your life. Some typical strategies to manage stress include aromatherapy, exercise, napping, journaling, and breathing exercises.

#14: Manage Your Expectations

We all have expectations for ourselves and other people. We even have expectations for things and animals. With expectations come satisfaction and disappointment. If our expectations are met, we become happy, if they're not, we become disappointed and possibly angry. We expect from ourselves, family members, friends, coworkers, and even strangers to behave a certain and when that doesn't happen, we become angry, because anger is just dissatisfaction with reality. But it's absurd to expect all people and all circumstances to be as they should. This is why we must learn to set realistic expectations, so we don't set ourselves up to be disappointed and frustrated.

#15: Create a Kit

Use a "calm down" kit to help you relax or control your temper. Think about objects that help you engage your thoughts and senses because looking, seeing, touching, smelling, or hearing calm things, make it easy to change your emotional state. Create a "calm down" kit with the following items:

- A happy photo of you with your family
- Scented hand lotion or candle
- Mood-boosting essential oils like bergamot and lavender
- A soothing message written on a piece of paper
- Your "why" written on a piece of paper
- A picture of a serene landscape
- Some candy
- A stress relief ball

The point is to include things that can help calm your nerves and make you feel better. Keep these items close to you for easy access.

#16: Communicate Effectively

Most arguments that lead to frustration and anger are caused by miscommunications. Improving your communication skills will allow you to better express your feelings and intentions and prevent any misunderstandings. It'll also allow you to better understand people and accept their viewpoints so you can prevent unjustified anger.

#17: Knowledge is Power

Read books, watch videos, and sign up for courses on anger management. Learn as much as you can. The more aware you become, the more you'll be empowered to act and change with confidence. The more anger management tools and tricks you discover, the more prepared you'll be to overcome anger. Knowledge drives action and gives you better control of your life.

#18: Join Support Groups Online

To help you better deal with your anger on your own, join support groups online. There are many free anger management groups you can find on Facebook. These are groups where people dealing with similar issues come together to support and share coping strategies and resources. These groups are great for encouragement, comfort, and advice.

#19: Ask for Professional Help

If you're concerned about your anger issues and how they're affecting you and the people around you, then you should look into seeking professional help. Sign up for an anger management course in your area or online, or book an appointment with a therapist. The American Psychological Association has an online guide for finding psychologists. You can find this guide with a quick google search. With the right support, guidance, and techniques, you'll be able to develop a plan to control your anger once and for all.

So how do you know when to seek professional help? Here are some common signs that you should consider:

- Being violent with people, objects and yourself
- Getting in constant trouble with the law because of anger
- Not remembering what happened after an outburst

- Inward aggression
- Regularly starting fights with people

Immediate/Short-Term Strategies

This section covers some simple strategies you can use to control your temper in the "heat of the moment."

#20: Stop Talking

In the state of anger, you'll be tempted to scream, swear, or insult the person that upset you. When you're frustrated like this, pretend your lips are sealed shut. If you don't say anything, you won't have anything to regret. Keeping quiet will help you collect your thoughts and think about a healthier way to respond.

#21: Step Away

When you remain in front of your trigger, your anger will intensify. One of the easiest things to do to calm yourself down is to disengage from the situation. As soon as the conversation begins to escalate, step away. If you're in a meeting room, excuse yourself and go to the restroom. If you're with your partner, children, or someone you know, ask them to give you a break. Explain to them that you're working on managing your anger and that you need to step away; and that although you want to have a productive conversation, it won't be possible when you're angry.

#22: Take a Deep Breath

When angry, you start taking quick shallow breaths from your chest. You can counteract this with controlled deep breaths to return your breathing to normal. Take a few moments to focus on your breathing as you inhale deeply through your nose and exhale through your mouth making sure to let all the air out. This will help you slow down your heart rate and feel more relaxed.

#23: Relax your Muscles

Your muscles can become tight after an episode of anger. This tension is usually in the neck, shoulders, and back. Use the progressive muscle relaxation technique to focus your thoughts on the tension in your body and then release it. To use this technique, tighten one of the tense muscles, hold it for 10 seconds while breathing, then relax the muscle. Do this for each tense muscle. This tightening and relaxing of the muscles will slowly release the tension and feelings of anger.

#24: Visualize

Go to a quiet room, close your eyes, and breathe deeply. Visualize yourself in a relaxing and serene landscape. Focus your thoughts on every detail in the comforting scenery. Are you by the beach? How does the sand feel? What sounds can you hear? This is another great exercise for de-escalating anger.

You can use the last three relaxation techniques anywhere, even around people. If something at work frustrates you, for example, you can discreetly use these techniques to let go of the stress quickly without needing to go to a different room. However, keep in mind that it does take time to master these exercises. You have to commit and practice them continuously to see their benefits.

#25: Use the Stop Sign

What do we all instinctively do when we approach a stop sign? We stop...or at least we should. It's become embedded in our minds that this symbol means stop. So why not use this to our advantage during a fit of anger. Simply imagine a stop sign when you see yourself getting worked up. This should allow you to stop your racing thoughts and buy you some time to reconsider your reaction. Use those quick moments to also consider what will be the consequences of your actions if you lose your temper.

#26: Use Relaxing Images

Use your cherished memories of your friends and family to put yourself in a better mood. Carry a picture of your partner, parents, children, or pets in your wallet and look at them when you're angry. This will help you relax and regain control of your emotions.

#27: Count in Your Head

Depending on how angry you are, start counting to 10 or a 100. If you want to make it a little more challenging, count down. This allows your heart rate to slow down and distracts your thoughts away from the stressful situation. It buys you time to better control your reaction to the trigger.

#28: Go Exercise

Research shows that exercise quickly reduces anger and calms one's nerves. Perform any activity that gets your heart pumping and shifts your focus away from your triggers. Go for a jog, play basketball, or go swimming to blow off some steam.

#29: Stretch

Perform simple movements and stretches that don't require any equipment. Although less strenuous than exercise, stretching will distract you from your emotions and help relax your muscles. Since the shoulders, neck, and arms tend to tighten when angry, try to stretch them out with shoulder and neck rolls.

#30: Repeat a Calming Phrase

Find a phrase or word that helps you refocus and feel relaxed. Repeat that phrase and word until your anger subsides. It could be something like: "You will be fine," "relax," and "you're in control." Take a moment now to come up with your own calming phrase and practice saying it.

#31: Timeout

Give yourself a time out to get away from everybody. Take a walk by yourself to relax and process everything that happened. This time away from people will help you collect your composure and think over things. You can even take this a step further and add it to your daily schedule. It'll be your special time to reflect on your emotions, triggers, and plans for how to respond to stressful events.

#32: Time it

To help you think before acting, set a timer. Decide how long you want to wait before you respond or do something. Then when you find yourself angry, start the timer. Doing this will buy you extra time to get your anger under control and make better decisions.

#33: Get Creative

Try painting, knitting, or pottery and use your anger's energy to produce something special and unpredictable. Creativity has been proven to reduce anger because it requires focus and physical movement which distracts your mind away from what made you angry. Any activity that absorbs your attention is always a good way to treat anger.

#34: Take a Shower

Wash your face or take a shower to relax and distance yourself from the issue. It will refresh your body and put you in a better mood.

#35: Journal

Use journaling to release your emotions and help you ease your anger. The simple act of expressing your feelings in some form is enough to make you feel better. Keep it close so you can make daily notes of stressful situations, how you felt, and your reactions. This can help you evaluate what happened and prevent internalizing anger.

#36: Talk to Someone

In the grip of anger, your good judgment will be clouded, and it will be difficult to think logically about what happened. This is why it's always a good idea to talk to someone you trust, whether a friend or a family member. It will help you get over your frustration by looking at the situation from a different angle. In addition, the act of talking to a caring person about your problems is in itself therapeutic.

#37: Force a Smile or Laugh

The simple act of smiling is enough to change our entire mood. Research has shown that smiling makes us happier while scowling make's angrier. Laughter has an even greater effect. It reduces stress and releases endorphins to make us feel good. You can quickly diffuse anger and feel better by having a good laugh. Try watching or reading something funny.

#38: Imagine Seeing Yourself Angry

Imagine looking at yourself in an angry state. How you would look and act? Imagine seeing your red bulging eyes, your veins popping out on your forehead as you scream at someone. Would you be pleased to look at that or want someone else to see that? I doubt it. Next time you're about to lose your temper on someone, picture how you would look.

#39: Be Grateful

Instead of focusing on what is wrong, focus on what is right. Don't dwell on negativity. Reflect on the countless blessings in your life. Remember the times where you successfully kept your composure and restrained yourself from getting angry. Realizing the good things around you and what you've done right, can help neutralize your feelings and change your perspective on things.

#40: Forgive

Find the courage to forgive the individual who wronged you. Let go of resentment and grudges. Don't hang on the hurtful words and allow bitterness to cloud your judgment. Remember that everyone has flaws and will make mistakes. Don't emphasize their flaws but focus instead on their good qualities. Forgiving is not easy and takes a lot of practice, but once mastered it will help you live a stress-free life.

#41: Be Empathetic

Put yourself in the other person's shoes. Try considering their feelings, thoughts, and perspective, you 'll be able to understand and forgive them. Also, make excuses for them. For example, imagine on your way home while driving on the highway, someone dangerously cuts you off. It's completely natural for anybody in this instance to become enraged because of the fact this person could've killed them. But instead of getting angry, you make an excuse or excuses for her and tell yourself: maybe she didn't see me, or maybe she's got an injured person in the car that she's rushing to the hospital or maybe it was my fault.

Quick Summary:

- **Anger Management:** It teaches one to identify his or her triggers and warning signs and provides healthy methods for expressing anger.

- Use long term strategies such as creating an anger management plan, exercising, getting enough sleep, and eating well to permanently cope with anger and improve well-being.

- Use short term strategies to quickly regain control of your temper after an episode of anger. Some useful strategies include walking away, journaling, and relaxation techniques.

Chapter 7:
Specific Strategies

Dealing with Internalized Anger

Some people internalize their anger and shy away from expressing their frustration. Over time, this leads to psychological and physiological issues such as self-hate, depression, migraines, heart disease, cancer, and even suicidal thoughts. This form of anger is tremendously self-destructive. People suffering from this turn their anger inward and continuously criticize and blame themselves. As a result of this, they inflict self-harm and abuse. Because of the tension and anger they've bottled up, they're sometimes abusive to others as well. To deal with internalized or self-abusive anger, a person needs to learn to manage his or her anger with general as well as specific techniques meant for coping with internalized anger. Below are some of these specific strategies.

#42: Accept Your Problem

The first step is to acknowledge your problem for what it is—relentless self-abuse— so that you can focus on fixing it. Once you realize the amount of harm you've been afflicting on yourself, you'll have the motivation to change.

#43: Be Self-Compassionate

Be easy on yourself and practice self-compassion. This should be easy after accepting the fact that you've been a victim of your own abuse. Be understanding of your limits as a human being and make excuses for yourself when you fail or fall short of your expectations—nobody is perfect. This might not be easy at first, but studies have proven that self-compassion can be learned.

#44: Challenge the Negative Thoughts

Don't accept the hateful statements coming from your inner critic, challenge, and reject them. Take a deep breath and pause your racing mind for a moment to think about the reality of the situation, is it in line with these negative feelings? Are these fair judgments? Whenever you notice these negative thoughts creeping up, stop them in their tracks, and question them. A similar way of dealing with negative self-talk is to simply stop it. Ignore it and don't even entertain it in your head. Distract yourself instead with positive thoughts.

#45: List Your Strengths

Write down your strengths, good qualities, and accomplishments on a piece of paper. It will make you feel better, increase your self-esteem, and better equip you to fight off the negative critic inside of you. When you notice self-hate thoughts starting up, get your piece of paper out, and read your good qualities and accomplishments out load.

#46: Don't Isolate Yourself

The self-hate thoughts might make you believe that no one wants to be around you, but this is not true just like all the other self-hate statements. Withdrawing from all of your friends and family members will only make things worse. Hang out with the people that you love; they'll make you feel better. Part of being human is our need to be around other people, it makes us feel loved and important. Don't let your negative critic convince you otherwise.

If you find that your internalized anger is taking over and you're not able to cope with it by yourself, speak to a professional. As mentioned previously, the American Psychological

Association has a great online tool that can help you find the right therapist for you.

Dealing with Anger in a Relationship

How couples react or respond to anger and frustration can make or break a relationship. Since anger is a natural response and is present in every relationship, it's a must that both partners in any relationship learn to express it constructively. The following strategies will help you better communicate with your partner and relieve tension.

#47: Don't Ignore Your Partner

As you know, remaining silent is key to regaining your composure, but in a relationship, you have to consider the other person's feelings. You can't just ignore your partner and walk away; it'll only escalate their anger. You have to let them know that you're remaining quiet and giving yourself some space to cool down and collect your thoughts.

#48: Resist Blaming

No one likes to get blamed, especially when in a state of anger. Avoid blaming your partner at all costs, it only makes things worse and could have long-lasting effects on your relationship. When you criticize someone, you're attacking that person's character, so how do you think that's going to make them feel? Do you think they'll accept your point? Definitely not! If you can't resist the urge to blame, then just stop talking and excuse yourself. Wait until you're both calmer to get your point across in a constructive way.

#49: Work on Yourself First

In relationships, mistreatment is reciprocal. If you use verbal aggression towards your spouse, expect the same from her. If you want your spouse to change her negative behaviors, you need to change yours first. Remember that you're not perfect, so how can you expect her to be without flaws? Ultimately, we can't change how others feel or behave, but we can change ourselves, and set good examples for people to follow.

#50: Don't Take It Personally

Your loved one could be angry for many reasons and you might not be the cause at all. Focus on making her feel better and remove yourself emotionally from the situation. Sometimes our loved ones just need to vent and we're the only ones around that they can talk to.

#51: Let Them Vent

If you notice your partner getting riled up, pause, and listen to their concerns without judging or inserting your opinion. Give them a chance to express themselves. This is therapeutic and will help them relieve their frustration. Let them know you understand why they're frustrated. Once they've calmed down, continue the discussion, and express your feelings.

#52: Actively Listen

Show them you're listening to what they're saying and confirm their feelings. Repeat what they said to make sure you understood. Maintain eye contact and lean towards them to show that you care and want to make them feel better.

#53: Use Humor

Try telling a joke to change the mood. Humor has been proven to help diffuse tension between people. However, avoid using sarcasm as you could insult or further anger the person you're talking to.

Dealing with Anger at Work

It's easy to get frustrated at work and it happens to all of us from time to time. A habitually late coworker who leaves all the work for you or a controlling boss who's never happy with your performance is enough to get anybody boiling. Triggers like these can easily upset you and distract your focus away from your tasks if you don't know how to manage your anger properly. Here are some quick tips to help you better cope with frustration at work:

#54: End the Confrontation

Try to put some distance between yourself and the situation as soon as possible. Walk away or go outside and get some fresh air. Give yourself time to process the situation and to clear your head. When you do go back to the office, you'll be in a much better state to confront the person that you got into an angry exchange with.

#55: Plan Your Words

When you're ready to express your feelings to the person that upset you, carefully plan what you want to say to them and schedule a meeting. You want to communicate your thoughts professionally and assertively without offending them. If possible, ask them for their perspective of the situation and how they felt to better understand what happened. Suggest how you should deal with a similar situation next time. This kind of communication and dialogue will help you avoid misunderstandings in the future.

#56: Talk to a Colleague

If there's someone at work that you trust, confide in them. Ask them for their opinion on the situation. The act of telling someone how you feel helps to put things into perspective. Your trusted colleague can help you find a solution to resolve the issue with the person that you're angry with.

#57: Anger Won't Help

Recall the last time you lost your temper at work. Did it help fix the problem? Did it make it worse or had no effect at all? It's more than likely that it didn't solve anything, or it probably made things worse. So, there's no point in staying angry, it's best to just force yourself to get over it and focus your thoughts on something else.

#58: Distract Yourself

If you find yourself boiling with anger, quickly disrupt it by busying yourself with a calming activity. You could go through your social media, play a game on your phone, or practice the relaxation techniques mentioned before such as deep breathing and progressive muscle relaxation. You could also call a loved one to cheer you up.

#59: Schedule Recharge Breaks

It's normal for everybody to have energy slumps while at work. For most people, it's usually around noon. And when we're overcome with fatigue, we're more irritable and likely to get angry, so it's best to schedule recharge breaks when this happens. Identify when you feel most drained at work and then plan your break accordingly. Take a walk or have a snack. Make sure to avoid anyone or situation that might frustrate you.

#60: Don't Multitask

Studies have shown that multitasking can lead to stress, anxiety, and a feeling of being overwhelmed and lowered productivity. These feelings can then cause frustration and anger. To prevent this, simply avoid multi-tasking. Focus all your energy on one task so you don't feel rushed or overwhelmed. You'll make better decisions and produce quality work while keeping your composure.

Quick Summary:

- **Tips for dealing with internalized anger include:**

1. Accept your self-abuse problem.
2. Practice self-compassion.
3. Challenge your negative thoughts.

- **Tips for dealing with anger in a relationship include:**

1. Don't ignore.
2. Don't blame.
3. Use humor.

- **Tips for dealing with anger at work include:**

1. End the confrontation.
2. Carefully plan what you want to say to them.
3. Distract yourself.

Chapter 8:
Confronting Angry People

So far, we've looked at different methods and strategies to help you control your anger. However, we also have to consider the other side – dealing with angry people. Most of us work or deal with angry people daily, and these interactions can be quite draining. In this section, we'll go over a few tips you can use to confront angry people and de-escalate a situation. People express anger differently. Some may internalize it by withdrawing or being sarcastic, while others may scream, insult, or get physical. This means that you need to vary the way you'll deal with the different anger expressions.

Maintain a Calm Demeanor

Don't respond with anger, it'll just add fuel to the fire. Try to keep your voice calm even if you're angry inside. Use non-threatening body language to show that you're willing to listen to what they have to say. Lower your voice and speak calmly. This can help prompt the other person to lower their voice. Keeping your composure like this can make the angry person realize his error and come back to his senses or walk away when he notices that you have no interest in arguing with him.

Don't Insult Them

Insulting an angry person is a sure way to make their anger worse. Avoid any words that might offend them, even general words like "never," or "always." Try to use positive words as much as possible. Instead of saying, "why do you **always** yell at me?" say, "please don't yell at me." These subtle changes can ensure that the person doesn't feel attacked. You can express your disagreements to them after they've cooled off and are in a better mood to accept criticism.

Know When to End it

If a person is so upset that she can't hold a reasonable discussion, disengage. Continuing the argument might only escalate her anger. Tell her that you can continue talking when you've both in a happier mood. If you don't know the person, then apologize for your role in the situation and excuse yourself from the conversation.

Give Them Space

This is one of the best things you can do to help an upset person cool down. Give them space and time to get their anger under control. Let them approach you when they're ready.

Be Safe

Some people become physically aggressive when they become enraged. If you know the angry person to have this tendency, then for your safety, remove yourself from the situation as fast as possible. If you don't have a choice but to be around this person, have a plan in place to get yourself out safely. Or ensure that you always have someone with you when you're around them.

Quick Summary:

- **Tips for dealing with angry people include:**

  1. Stay calm.
  2. Don't insult them.
  3. Disengage when necessary.

Chapter 9:
What If the Techniques Don't Work?

People are different and have different forms of anger, so some techniques may work for some but not others. No one method works for everybody which is why I tried to list as many techniques as possible so you can pick and choose from them as you like. Make sure to create a control plan using a strategy that is most suited to you and your situation and try to master it. Stick to it for at least a week before switching to try a different strategy; because learning to manage anger is a habit and habits take some to time form, we just have to be consistent with them.

If the strategy doesn't work for you, it's completely fine, just try a different one. Don't let minor setbacks make you give you up. You might have a very good week in controlling your temper but may lash out at somebody the following week. That's okay, it's part of the process of building new habits.

Pitfalls to Avoid

To help you ensure that your anger management plan works effectively, avoid these pitfalls:

1. React to triggers without thinking
2. Explode with anger over every minor annoyance
3. Ignore stress
4. Suppress anger
5. Allow your anger to build up
6. Hang on to hurtful words
7. Hold grudges
8. Replay negative situations in your head
9. Entertain negative self-hate thoughts
10. Take remarks personally
11. Venting on objects like pillows
12. Driving while angry
13. Not getting enough sleep

If You Get Angry

When you do slip and lose your temper, here are a couple of tips to help you better cope and resolve the situation:

Apologize

Apologizing is really effective in diffusing a heated argument or situation. Genuinely apologize to the person you lashed out at, it might not be easy, but it shows your strength and ability to swallow your pride—and you'll be appreciated for it. Let your friends and family members know that you're working on your anger issues so they can be more understanding and supportive of your anger management goals.

Remember to Forgive Yourself

Learning to manage anger doesn't happen overnight. It takes time and patience. When you do fail and lose your temper, remind yourself that you're still learning. Forgive yourself and don't let the negative thoughts lower your morale.

Assess the Situation

Review your anger log and think about what went wrong. Did you not catch your warning signs? Did you forget to use an anger management strategy? Was the strategy ineffective? Whatever the cause was, learn from it so that you can plan better going forward.

Quick Summary:

- Stick to your anger control plan and test different techniques to see which ones work best for you.

- **Common pitfalls to avoid include:**

    1. Reacting without thinking first.
    2. Suppressing anger
    3. Taking comments personally
    4. Not getting enough sleep

- **Tips for when you lose your anger:**

    1. Apologize to the person you got upset with.
    2. Forgive yourself.
    3. Assess the situation and learn from it.

- Don't let small setbacks deter you, it's part of the journey, keep going.

Conclusion

Congratulations on reading through to here, we're almost done! Knowing what you know now, you should feel confident and empowered to face your daily triggers with complete control and composure. Changing the bad habit of anger is not easy, but with the correct mindset, hard work, and tools, you can do it.

To quickly recap, remember these crucial steps for managing anger:

1. Identify your "Why."
2. Identify your triggers and early warning signs (physical and emotional).
3. Plan and apply an appropriate strategy.
4. Assess your reaction to the trigger. Build on your successes and plan better from the failures.
5. Be patient with the process.

Throughout this book, you've expanded your understanding of anger and learned why as well as how you should deal with it. You've also discovered over 60 simple strategies to help you control your temper in different situations as well as strategies for confronting an angry person. Let's quickly summarize them so you can easily refer to them at any time:

Quick List of Anger Management Strategies

Preventative Strategies to Manage Anger:

1. Become aware of your anger
2. Identify your "why"
3. Learn your triggers & signs
4. Make anger management goals
5. Create an anger control plan
6. Practice how you want to respond to triggers
7. Track your progress in an anger log
8. Control your negative thoughts
9. Reward yourself when you succeed
10. Exercise regularly
11. Eat well
12. Sleep well
13. Manage your stress
14. Set realistic expectations
15. Create a calming kit
16. Communicate effectively
17. Learn more about anger management
18. Join support groups online
19. Ask for professional help

Immediate Strategies to Manage Anger:

20. Stop talking
21. Step away
22. Take deep breaths
23. Relax your muscles
24. Visualize a calming scene
25. Picture the stop sign
26. Look at relaxing images
27. Count in your head
28. Go exercise
29. Stretch
30. Repeat a calming phrase
31. Give yourself a timeout
32. Set a timer for when you want to act
33. Get creative
34. Take a shower
35. Journal
36. Talk to someone
37. Force a smile or laugh
38. Imagine seeing yourself angry
39. Be grateful
40. Forgive
41. Be empathetic

Strategies for Managing Internalized Anger:

42. Accept your self-hate problem
43. Be self-compassionate

44. Challenge the negative thoughts
45. List your strengths and read them out loud
46. Don't isolate yourself

Strategies for Managing Anger in a Relationship:

47. Don't ignore your partner
48. Resist blaming
49. Work on yourself first
50. Don't take it personally
51. Let your partner vent
52. Actively listen
53. Use humor

Strategies for Dealing with Anger at Work:

54. End the confrontation
55. Plan your words
56. Talk to a colleague about it
57. Remember that anger won't help
58. Distract yourself
59. Schedule recharge breaks
60. Don't multitask

Strategies for Dealing with Angry People:

61. Maintain a calm demeanor
62. Don't insult them
63. Know when to end it

64. Give them space to cool down
65. Stay safe

I hope the information in this book will empower you to overcome your anger so that you can live a stress-free life full of joy and great moments with your loved ones.

What next? I want you to take action right now—go and create an anger control plan with one of these strategies. Remember that it's okay to slip occasionally, be patient with the process of improving your life. To make this journey easier, make sure to use the free Anger Control Plan and Anger Log templates I've provided for you. You can download them here if you haven't already:

https://tinyurl.com/free-anger-control-plan

Thanks for Reading

How'd you enjoy reading this book? I hope you got tons of value from it. I want to thank you again for purchasing my book and taking the time to read it, it REALLY means a lot to me.

If you've enjoyed reading it and found some benefit in it, I'd love to hear from you, as it'll help me to ensure that I improve this book and others in the future.

So, please do take a minute to leave a review of this book on Amazon.

I want to let you know that your review is very important to me and will help this book reach and impact more people's lives.

Thank you so much for your time and support!

It's been a pleasure,

A.B. Alin

Printed in Great Britain
by Amazon

73428470R00054